Echolocations

THE NICHOLAS ROERICH POETRY PRIZE

is an annual first-book competition sponsored by
the Nicholas Roerich Museum in New York City
www.storylinepress.com

The Volcano Inside by David Dooley   1988

Without Asking by Jane Ransom   1989

Death, But at a Good Price by Chris Semansky   1990

The Buried Houses by David Mason   co-winners
Desire's Door by Lee McCarthy   1991

30 Miles from J-Town by Amy Uyematsu   1992

House Without a Dreamer by Andrea Hollander Budy   1993

Counterpoint by David Alpaugh   1994

The Silent Partner by Greg Williamson   1995

Infidelities by Elise Paschen   1996

The Laws of Falling Bodies by Kate Light   co-winners
January Rain by Daniel Anderson   1997

The Long Home by Christian Wiman   1998

An Honest Answer by Ginger Andrews   1999

Echolocations

poems by

Diane Thiel

Winner of the 13th Annual Nicholas Roerich Poetry Prize

Story Line Press
Ashland, Oregon

Published by Story Line Press, Three Oaks Farm, PO Box 1240, Ashland OR 97520-0055

This publication was made possible thanks in part to the generous support of the Nicholas Roerich Museum, the Andrew W. Mellon Foundation, The Collins Foundation, the Rose E. Tucker Charitable Trust, the Oregon Arts Commission, and our individual contributors.

Front cover painting by Salvador Dali
Archeological Reminiscence of Millet's Angelus
(1933-35) Oil on panel
12 1/2 x 15 1/2 inches
Collection of The Salvador Dali Museum
St. Petersburg, Florida
Copyright 2000 by Salvador Dali Museum, Inc.
Author photo by Costa Hadjilambrinos
Book design by Lysa McDowell
Composition by Wellstone Publications

Library of Congress Cataloging-in-Publication Data

Thiel, Diane, 1967-
   Echolocations: poems / Diane Thiel.
     p. cm.
   "Winner of the 13th annual Nicholas Roerich poetry prize."
   ISBN 1-58654-002-5 (cloth) — ISBN 1-885266-97-9 (alk. paper)

   I. Title

PS3570.H4418 E28 2000
811'.6—cd21   00-056292

ACKNOWLEDGMENTS

My thanks to the editors of the following journals, where these poems first appeared: *American Poets and Poetry:* "Miami Circle "; *Blueline:* "Catwalk," "Circumstance"; *Coal City Review:* "The Hollows," "Legacies," "Exposure"; *The Dark Horse* (Scotland): "Memento Mori in Middle School," "Family Album," "Echolocations"; *Fireweed:* "Quilt"; *The Great Stream Review:* "The River Blued"; *Gulfstream:* "Letters from the Garden III and IV"; *The Hudson Review:* "Twelve-Day Buddhist Silent Retreat"; *Kalliope:* "Killdeer," "Bluefield, West Virginia"; *Loonfeather:* "Belongings"; *Mandrake Poetry Review:* "Bedside Readers, "Perception," "Swallow," "Crossroads"; *Mangrove:* "South Beach Wedding"; *Next Phase:* "Silences"; *Notre Dame Review:* "Changeling"; *Poetry:* "Kinderund Hausmärchen," "Trümmerfrauen," "Love Letters"; *Red Cedar Review:* "Measurements"; *Smartish Pace:* "Textiles," "Prefix," "Legacy," "Poetry"; *SnowApple:* "Träume"; *So to Speak:* "Isla de la Luna"; *Sundog: The Southeast Journal:* "Sunshine Families"; *Timber Creek Review:* "Florida Turnpike"; *Tor House Newsletter:* "The Minefield"; *Whiskey Island Magazine:* "Watermark." The following are scheduled to appear: *The Dark Horse:* "At the Mailbox"; *Louisiana Literature:* "Delineations," "Miami Beach," "The Harvest"; *Willow Springs:* "Excavations".

Best American Poetry 1999 re-printed "The Minefield." *Beacon Best of 2000* re-printed "Family Album." "Tea" appeared in the *1999 Emily Dickinson Award Anthology*. "Geologic" and "In the Thirtieth Year" have been selected for *Troubador Best of Rhyme 2001*. "The Minefield" will also be re-printed in *Poetry: an Introduction*, 3rd edition (Bedford/St. Martin's) and *The Bedford Introduction to Literature*, 6th edition. "Memento Mori in Middle School" will be re-printed in *An Introduction to Poetry*, 10th edition (Addison, Wesley, Longman). My gratitude to the editors of these anthologies.

The following poems have appeared in on-line publications: *Ablemuse:* "History's Stories," "South Beach Wedding," "Wilderness," "Moment," "Thera," "Event Horizons," "After Basho"; *Poetry Daily:* "Twelve-Day Buddhist Silent Retreat" (selected from *The Hudson Review*); *PoetryNet/* Poet of the Month: re-published "Love Letters," "Memento Mori," "History's Stories," "Echolocations"; *Torhouse.org:* "Crossing." I thank the editors.

"For Pyramus," "Calculations," "Family Album," "Tea," and "Distance" appeared as a limited edition chapbook: *Cleft in the Wall*, from Aralia Press, 1999. "Echolocations" was re-printed as a single-poem chapbook in the Aralia Solo Voices series, 2000. I appreciate the beautiful work of Michael Peich, Director of Aralia Press, and his fellow artisans.

The title poem received the 1999 Robert Frost Award for Poetry from the Frost Foundation. "Memento Mori in Middle School" was the co-winner of the 2000 *New Millennium Writings* Award IX and was reprinted in the award issue. "The Minefield" received the 1998 Robinson Jeffers Award for Poetry from Tor House Foundation. "Isla de la Luna" received the 1999 *So to Speak* Award for Poetry (2nd place) from George Mason University. A selection of poems received the 1990 Judith Siegel Pearson Award for Poetry from Wayne State University. My gratitude to the associations which presented these awards.

Many individuals have encouraged these poems and helped bring them into being. My thanks to friends, colleagues, students, editors and other influences too numerous to name. For various forms of inspiration and help in bringing forth this book, I would particularly like to thank Greg Brown, Corina Dueñas, Donald Hall, Michael Hettich, Mark Jarman, Janet Konefal, Kathryn Kruger, David Mason, Ana Maria Tierra, Anthony Walton, and Christian Wiman. Special thanks to Fred D'Aguiar, Dana Gioia, Michael Harper, and Robert McDowell for their extraordinary support. Finally, my deep gratitude is acknowledged in the dedication of this book.

For my family, old and new,
and especially for Costa,
matia mu.

CONTENTS

I. Kinder- und Hausmärchen

II. Memento Mori

III. Distance

IV. The River Blued

'Time to plant tears,' says the almanac.
The grandmother sings to the marvelous stove
and the child draws another inscrutable house.

—Elizabeth Bishop

When lightning blasted her nest she built it again on the same tree, in the splinters of the thunderbolt...

...at night the rock slides rattle and thunder in the throats of these living mountains.

—Robinson Jeffers

I.

Kinder- und Hausmärchen

Kinder- und Hausmärchen

tiefere Bedeutung
Liegt in dem Märchen meiner Kinderjahre
Als in der Wahrheit, die das Leben lehrt.
            —Friedrich Schiller

deeper meaning
lies in the fairy tales of my childhood
than in the truth that life teaches.

Saint Nikolaus had a giant gunny sack
to put the children in if they were bad.
It was a hole so deep you'd never come back.
A porch swing full of stories, where the smoke
went up in hot, concentric, perfect rings
and filled our heads with unbelievable things.

A nursery heavy with a history
where nothing was whatever it had seemed,
where Aschenputtel's sisters cut their feet
half off—so desperate they were to fit.
And in the end, they also lost their eyes
when steel-grey birds descended from the skies.

Rotkäppchen's wolf was someone that she knew,
who wooed her with a man's words in the woods.
But she escaped. It always struck me most
how Grandmother, whose world was swallowed whole,
leapt fully formed out of the wolf alive.
Her will came down the decades to survive

in mine—my heart still desperately believes
the stories where somebody re-conceives
herself, emerges from the hidden belly,
the warring home dug deep inside the city.
We live today those stories we were told.
Es war einmal im tiefen tiefen Wald.

The Minefield

He was running with his friend from town to town.
They were somewhere between Prague and Dresden.
He was fourteen. His friend was faster
and knew a shortcut through the fields they could take.
He said there was lettuce growing in one of them,
and they hadn't eaten all day. His friend ran a few lengths ahead,
like a wild rabbit across the grass,
turned his head, looked back once,
and his body was scattered across the field.

My father told us this, one night,
and then continued eating dinner.

He brought them with him—the minefields.
He carried them underneath his good intentions.
He gave them to us—in the volume of his anger,
in the bruises we covered up with sleeves.
In the way he threw anything against the wall—
a radio, that wasn't even ours,
a melon, once, opened like a head.
In the way we still expect, years later and continents away,
that anything might explode at any time,
and we would have to run on alone
with a vision like that
only seconds behind.

Delineations

Kind, du fragst mir Löcher im Bauch,
his father often told him after the war,
collecting his remaining children, moving
west of the Oder, and then west of the Elbe.
Among my father's favorite possessions
were turn-of-the-century maps his father left him.
The maps would give some answers to our questions.
He'd let us use the magnifying glass—
he'd trace his finger over old Silesia,
start talking to himself, as if in trance:

"This might have been the house—and this, the farm.
This thin red line, the road I walked to town.
I think the last time was to say goodbye
to Tante Grete when I went to Prague
for school. She always said to me, *Verfahr
dich nicht.* When you're a kid, you never think
you can't go home again—Imagine trying
to cross the state line into Florida
when you come home from summer camp one year,
but there's a sign that says *Stop. No Access.*"

But if we ever asked a direct question,
to get him, just for once, to finish a thought,
we'd watch the curtain drop. He'd close the maps
inside their tattered, yellow folder, saying
Kind, du fragst mir Löcher im Bauch.

Changeling

Bernhard had nothing but their names.
He'd come there on his own.
He asked and asked, but no one knew.
So many had come and gone.

The boy had followed others west
and walked much of the way.
In the leveled continent,
Dresden had been saved.

The city was filled with refugees
when the markers floated down,
cone-shaped like Christmas trees
lighting up the ground.

For this—the city had been saved,
the people suddenly knew.
They poured into their cellars. Someone
brought the boy below.

Beneath the ground, he couldn't see
the rain of fire fall,
but he could hear each bomb explode
and feel the buildings crumble.

The heat melted all it touched,
bodies before the stones,
carving out the Frauenkirche
down to her catacombs.

Between three raids that night and day,
survivors left their cellars
and faced the burning homes next door
caved in at their centers.

The streets were heavy with rock and ash
as another search began—
turning over coats to find them
holding skeletons.

Alone in the hollowed city, Father
wrote on the church in chalk:
Where are you, Paul and Hedel Thiel?
I live. Bernhard

Textiles

What did I know, what did I know
of love's austere and lonely offices?
                              —Robert Hayden

We found the bolt of thick purple cloth on the shore
at sunrise—we were always finding things
the ocean had brought in, but never anything like this.
We brought it home, unrolled it through the backyard
and into the front, like something royal.
It dried quickly in the noonday sun.

Then we swept it free of sand and salt.
We debated whether or not to cut it,
but we'd never get it clean unless we did.
The first layer was marked with tar. We cut it off
and measured the rest in equal parts,
washed, dried, and folded them.

"They'll make such perfect covers,
one for each of you," my father said.
He had been so different that day,
like a small boy having found a treasure.
When he came in to tell us a story that night,
he smoothed our new covers, fingering the cloth.

After he left, I lay thinking of the boy
half a life ago, hiding alone
in the Lausitz forest just east of Dresden.
The fresh rabbit skin as a pillow,
for a cover, the white parachute silk
that had likely floated down the flares before the bombs.

And what he chose to speak about, that time—how soft it was,
like nothing he had ever felt—he said,
it was such beautiful material.

Trümmerfrauen

I.

When the sirens began, we went underground,
and when we surfaced, the streets were gone.
The war gave us the name. Later,
when the men who lived were still in prison,
the women were left to clean everything up.

We collected the houses, churches, hospitals,
the halls where I had never danced,
impossible to sort. We all did something.
One woman pulled stone after stone from the rubble.
One hammered mortar from the edges.

One stacked bricks in orderly piles
next to the mountains—*Trümmerbergen.*
The rubble became part of so many words.
I remember a few *Trümmermänner,*
and long lines of *Trümmerkinder.*

II.

As a young woman not yet twenty,
I walked where my aunt had walked at that age,
clearing the nave of the Frauenkirche.
I spoke to an old couple nearby,
who said, "we don't talk about it."

We stood in silence. I could see the sky
through the windows of the two church walls—
sandstone forms, far from each other,
one worn column wearing its holes
like a place where the heart had been.

Träume

Whether you like it or not, your genes have a political past,
Your skin a political cast.
Whatever you say reverberates.
Whatever you don't say speaks for itself.
                    —Wislawa Szymborska

The language of our dreams contains
the places we can never name again
without the shame. Can we ever speak the words
Dachau, Buchenwald—the blighted patch
of Goethe's home on the banks of the Ilm,
the forest of books—burned with the bones.
It will take many lifetimes to reclaim
this language of my childhood.
In this recurring nightmare, I am dragging suitcases
behind me, filled with bodies, other selves
I silenced. The train pulled out again and again,
left the bags to be opened later and divided—

Like the genes in this body, remembering
more than they should know, learning
this white-washed language coating tongues
in hallways, smoking rooms,
on the constant flicker of screens—
hearing the murmurings of a machine
we will not name, until our hands
become hammers, our ears recorders,
our mouths removed.
With all these words caught in my throat,
the most terrible ones I hear are in the way
we speak of history—*then* and *they*.

Prefix

Most of the grounds of the world's troubles
are matters of grammar.
                    —Michel de Montaigne

I remember first learning
that you could add *ver*
to change the meaning
of many German verbs—
laufen (to walk),
fahren (to drive),
could become *verlaufen*,
verfahren (to lose your way).
Like an incantation,
you could also add *ver* to nouns—
verfeinden (make an enemy)
vernichten (turn into nothing).
I remember first learning
that in my father tongue
were prefixes built in
to do everything wrong.

Love Letters

My mother wanted to learn some German
for my father and because her children
could already speak it a little.
She was tired of dusting the stacks of books
she couldn't read, tired of the letters
she always had to ask him to translate.

He was usually willing to translate
the cards his mother had written in German.
But sometimes there were other letters,
and when he read them to her and the children,
she had the same feeling she'd had with books
before she learned to read, when she was little.

She said it bothered her a little
that her own children would have to translate
for her, that they could pick up the same books
that were as Greek to her as they were German.
She started learning it from her children
and decided to leave my father letters.

She wrote my father daily love letters
and carefully placed them on the little
table where they put things for the children,
next to our favorite set of translations
of fairy tales we first heard in German.
She leaned one every day against his books,

the white paper stark beside the dark books.
But my father never answered her letters.
Instead, he returned them with his German
corrections in the margin, his little
red marks—hieroglyphs for her to translate,
as if she were one of the children.

Maybe she was just one of the children
in that house surrounded by rows of books.
Maybe her whole life was a translation
of what she imagined in the letters.
The space between them made her that little
girl, wandering lost inside the German.

Because her own children were half-German,
she built her life around those little books
translating the lines of her own letters.

Crossing

Da kommt man nimmer zum Grunde
—Robinson Jeffers

Five, or was it ten years old
on that dark blue night at sea,
you held tight to the railing,
listened to the sailor speak
of the unfathomable
bottom—that could never
be reached.

II.

Memento Mori

'Three dear things that women know,'
Sang a bone upon the shore.

— W. B. Yeats

Memento Mori in Middle School

When I was twelve, I chose Dante's *Inferno*
in gifted class—an oral presentation
with visual aids. My brother, *il miglior fabbro*,

said he would draw the tortures. We used ten
red posterboards. That day, for school, I dressed
in pilgrim black, left earlier to hang them

around the class. The students were impressed.
The teacher, too. She acted quite amused
and peered too long at all the punishments.

We knew by reputation she was cruel.
The class could see a hint of twisted forms
and asked to be allowed to round the room

as I went through my final presentation.
We passed the first one, full of poets cut
out of a special issue of *Horizon*.

The class thought these were such a boring set,
they probably deserved their tedious fates.
They liked the next, though—bodies blown about,

the lovers kept outside the tinfoil gates.
We had a new boy in our class named Paolo
and when I noted Paolo's wind-blown state

and pointed out Francesca, people howled.
I knew that more than one of us not-so-
covertly liked him. It seemed like hours

before we moved on to the gluttons, though,
where they could hold the cool fistfuls of slime
I brought from home. An extra touch. It sold

in canisters at toy stores at the time.
The students recognized the River Styx,
the logo of a favorite band of mine.

We moved downriver to the town of Dis,
which someone loudly re-named Dis and Dat.
And for the looming harpies and the furies,

who shrieked and tore things up, I had clipped out
the shrillest, most deserving teacher's heads
from our school paper, then thought better of it.

At the wood of suicides, we quieted.
Though no one in the room would say a word,
I know we couldn't help but think of Fred.

His name was in the news, though we had heard
he might have just been playing with the gun.
We moved on quickly by that huge, dark bird

and rode the flying monster, Geryon,
to reach the counselors, each wicked face,
again, I had resisted pasting in.

To represent the ice in that last place,
where Satan chewed the traitors' frozen heads,
my mother had insisted that I take

an ice-chest full of popsicles—to end
my gruesome project on a lighter note.
"It *is* a comedy, isn't it," she said.

She hadn't read the poem, or seen our art,
but asked me what had happened to the sweet,
angelic poems I once read and wrote.

The class, though, was delighted by the treat,
and at the last round, they all pushed to choose
their colors quickly, so they wouldn't melt.

The bell rang. Everyone ran out of school,
as always, yelling at the top of their lungs,
The *Inferno* fast forgotten, but their howls

showed off their darkened red and purple tongues.

Sunshine Families

When we played, we listened for your mother's
footsteps. What would she have said if she'd come in,
found two little girls stripping all the Barbies, Skippers,
Sunshine Families—the ones with too-wide eyes—
and foreign ones that had no TV name.
Ésa Diana, she'd blame it all on me,
even though she didn't know the half of it,
stories I brought across the street
of people walking naked in my house,
while you were told, at four, to "cover your *teticas*!"
We were a match, my house of no clear boundaries,
no doors between rooms, while yours all locked.

And later, your only instruction was
Éso no se la da a nadie.
That you don't give to anybody.

It came back the other day, watching your nieces.
Embarrassed, I recalled making one doll torture the other.
"But we didn't make them hurt *each other*,"
you reminded me. "We made them misbehave.
Then we punished them with twigs, shoelaces, our hands
half as big as their whole bodies. It never
left a mark. Except on one of them, we drew
bruises once that wouldn't wash off.
And remember—from then on,
she always had to be the bad one."

Calculations

My parents planned the five of us
with charts and waves and the little pain
my mother felt when ovulating.

She would even call my father home from work,
and say, "Come home, let's make the baby,"
if she thought it was the time.

My mother often told us this story,
as if having been wanted so much
was what mattered most.

I was born one month before I was expected.
She used to tease, "You were always in a hurry to leave.
You even came out early."

But sometimes I imagine all of their calculations
were wrong. The day my father came home
to make me with my mother, I was already there—

a tiny witness when he pushed inside her.
Caught in the dark mesh of their voices,
in the knead of their bodies,

I felt my mother's heart beat against me like a wing.

Family Album

I like old photographs of relatives
in black and white, their faces set like stone.
They knew this was serious business.
My favorite album is the one that's filled
with people none of us can even name.

I find the recent ones more difficult.
I wonder, now, if anyone remembers
how fiercely I refused even to stand
beside him for this picture—how I shrank
back from his hand and found the other side.

Forever now, for future family,
we will be framed like this, although no one
will wonder at the way we are arranged.
No one will ever wonder, since we'll be
forever smiling there—our mouths all teeth.

In the Thirtieth Year

In the thirtieth year of life
I took my heart to be my wife
                    —J.V. Cunningham

In the thirtieth year of life,
she took her heart to be a wife.

And as she turned her head at night
to quench the final candlelight,

the dreams that never crossed her lips
might have filled a thousand ships,

might have found a passage home,
and yet she sank them, stone by stone.

Wilderness

(after Louise Bogan)

Hidden in the house left clean
before the last note,
in the single bag carried
to the sudden airport,

in the memory of hands
that made her weak
is the wilderness that runs
but cannot speak.

Killdeer

She built her nest inside the muddy tracks
the truck had left after a night-long storm.
They hardened into grooves the depth of hands,
that spanned the narrow byway of the farm.

And every time we neared her secret mound,
she'd leave her nest and run to us like mad—
in circles, beat her wing against the ground
to steer us all away until we passed.

My mother said it must have been her first—
to build herself such an unlikely nest
and told us all to keep away from her
and let her get at least a moment's rest.

The Hollows

Back home, we called them hollers,
the clefts between the hills that sealed us off.
A voice could echo clear across the town.
Sometimes I asked about my little sister
in the one picture—Phyllis Ann, a year younger.
There was nothing wrong that anyone could see.

But she had been born with a hole in her spine.
Back then, there was nothing the doctor could do.
He said that, before the baby passed, her head would swell
and she'd die in her sleep within a few months.
Mama had to measure the baby's head
a few times—when it looked like it had swollen.

She was a good baby, everyone said.
Mama nursed her like the others, sang to her.
But once she put the baby down to sleep,
Mama was so scared to find her dead,
she wouldn't check on her until she cried.
Or she would wait until my father came home.

I was too little to remember the funeral.
Three months, nine days—said the stone with the lamb.
It was quick. It started raining. They finished
and came back from the small wet grave—to the car.
Mama said I looked at her across the seat,
with eyes like dark pools, deeper than my one year,

and crawled back in the hollow of her arms.

Bluefield, West Virginia

This farm has never had a well.
My ear pressed to the earth, I know
the sounds that fill this rabbit hole

begin a thousand feet below.
Our men are there to seek their worth.
They take the tiny birds and go

down each day. We stay, work the earth,
and feel the men beneath the ground
with every seed placed underneath

and every bird that cries out loud
as if it suddenly was freed.
And every song reminds us how

we might be next to dig that deep
grave—fall down this spiralling hole
to the dark city beneath our feet.

Quilt

At night this quiet covers me,
grown ragged on the center seam,
dividing all its history.

I touch the remnants—finely spun,
familiar pieces handed down
from chest to chest for far too long

to still remember what was cut,
that it was once a blouse, a skirt
she wore the night he took her heart.

I touch the fields I thought I knew
and smooth the places healed into
each other, at the ridges sewn

with careful secrets mouthed for all
the years she couldn't tell a soul.

III.

Distance

Permit me voyage, love, into your hands...
—Hart Crane

For Pyramus

We've been watching you over the garden wall
                    for hours.
The sky is darkening like a stain.
Something is going to fall like rain,
                    and it won't be flowers.
            —W.H. Auden

From somewhere within me, you heard this sound.
It might have been the groan of wind in the trees,
an unknown sound and yet familiar.

I have been on the outskirts of your secret
cleft in the garden wall. History absolves me
of the deed in advance, yet still holds me responsible.

My ferocious velvet sister, Thisbe, would kill for you,
while I am the one who wears these teeth,
this growl, and she is but a small thing.

The blood on this fallen shawl belongs
to neither of you, yet the mere sight is enough
to let your deepest fears—

While I wait back and watch the mulberry darken,
wearing only the evidence of survival on my face,
wondering at what I have begun.

I was not hungry when you chose to meet here,
merely curious, and your deep scent in the wind
something I would never devour.

Florida Turnpike

The angel in the house wants me to write
a love letter, to clean up all the words
which lie about our silent mouths in shards.
She wants me just to stop. Pull over now
and stop the truck.
                          The sun is going down,
and we were lost for hours, expected hours ago.
And how did that old saying go—least said?
Across the seat, I'm watching you move further
and further—you are miles away by now.

Near our exit, the car drives through a sea
of yellow butterflies crossing the highway.
I look at you to see if you have noticed
how fast we're moving—when the first one hits
the windshield with the impact of a fist.

Bedside Readers

Bukowski is not my favorite bedside read.
I've known one too many men who keep
a troubling volume tucked beside the bed,
in their apartments at the razor edge
of Terror Street and Agony Way,
where they keep Love, the dog from Hell, at bay
and let no daylight penetrate that lair.

And Larkin, there's another to beware
between the sheets, for all I like his form.
This be the verse to keep us all forewarned.
A life with Larkin would have made me dive
straight off that rocky coastal shelf—Believe
me this—unless you want a timely end,
Don't read your lover "Talking in Bed" in bed.

South Beach Wedding

On Saturday, we walked Miami Beach,
together searching any quiet streets
and came upon a church tucked in between
the Deco, where a little garden wedding
was being held. We couldn't help but move
a little closer. We must have been in love,
the way we neared to hear their vows—
                              CUT! CUT!
*Stop the scene! What's with the two of you? Can't
you see we're filming here? Security!*
The groom began to curse the summer heat.
The bride said she was melting in her dress.
Escorted firmly from the premises,
we heard the words ring out—*The Wedding Scene
take twenty-nine. Let's get it right this time!*

Belongings

You say every woman you've known is traveling
and face the common run—just before or after sleep hits,
you dream you see them all off, drive them one by one
to airports and train stations, help them take their leave.
You carry their trunks and boxes, navigate a thousand flights.

And when you wake, you do the necessary things—
joke about cutting the couch in two,
the love seat nobody wants, yet nobody wants to lose.
But what do you do—with the blue bowl,
smooth to the touch, that both of you loved?

It is easier to divide the things you came with.
You kneel together over the large brown trunk,
used for putting things away, or for traveling.
You talk only about the things you claim, everything
belonging to one person or another, even after years,

each thing saying—This is my heart. This is yours.

Perception

All she saw was how small he painted her
disappearing down the street,
through a dark valley of trucks and cars—
all she saw was how small he painted her.

Her tiny form blurred, but central like a fire,
burning long after the eye's heat—
what he painted was how long he watched her
disappearing down the street.

At the Mailbox

The first few times we met, our hearts would rise.
You must have thought that I had no excuse
since I am over a thousand times your size.
But ever since my brother introduced
the two of us, and showed his sibling love,
by catching you to put you in my hair—
I've had the kind that lizards can't get out of.
Now I tap the box to let you know I'm there,
a ritual we both appreciate.
Between my much awaited mail, you leave
your gifts. What would I do, if every day
my little house would open and receive
a mountain, where my living room once stood?
I'd move. At least, I like to think I would.

Measurements

She enters him moments before he enters her,
and she tells him she is doing so.
And in doing so, she is suddenly his,
but even more her own—

wishes like seeds she sprinkled long ago,
then spun them into yards and yards of hair
she dreamt she had cut for a single night
from another woman's head to finish her own,

to wear it down below her waist,
to wrap its darkness around her,
to hang from her window.
She measured her life each night,

just to know the lengths that she would go.

Moment

She recognized that moment, when a man
could want his life, could feel it come upon him
like something unexpected, rare, and borrowed
or found again, but certain to be lost.

The first time it returned in long enough
to let him know—we cannot choose to love,
to let her know that when he said, "Don't go—"
it was the moment he was speaking to.

Letters from the Garden

I.

I am finding poems stretching their limbs
inside these letters, a good bed for them
to wake in. Birds call and the day opens.

Half in dream, they are slowly taking form
in this long honey rhythm of the earth,
turning in its lovely gyre, again,

to kiss the morning sun, from all this way.

II.

I can see you kneeling in your garden,
feel the cool flesh of secret vegetables
hiding fully formed beneath the ground.
I can smell your stew simmering on the stove.

I can taste that bath you're drawing tonight,
hot hot water to let the fall blow in.
I can hear the timbre of your voice
in story after story of your life,

and feel the blush rise in my face and thighs,
and poems pouring, pouring down my hillside.

III.

I have been out looking for cypress trees,
ones behaving wickedly, their trunks
and branches stretched, their reddish knees exposed.

Do you remember the picture I sent you once
of the two trees that were really into it?
I found out later—one was a strangler fig.

But today, in this late afternoon light
in the glades, I found one tupelo, one cypress,
their hair thrown loose—fucking so slowly,

you could hardly see them move.

IV.

I want to show you the desert rose,
the coontie, blackberry, lignum vitae,
let you see where I was this morning,
on my hands and knees in the living dirt,
as living as the lady slipper trees.

I want to lie with you in this garden,
feel it cool around us when we become
this loam, as we have become every tree
you've loved me up against—
the earth full of us as we are full,

our seeds covered with the dark life of it.

Tea

My love reminds me of a great blue whale.
He moves like honey in this cup of tea,
his motions nearly imperceptible,
and yet he reaches both ends of the sea.
He sings a song he thinks I will not hear,
above the waves and on another coast.
And yet the echoes somehow reach my ear—
They travel through the mantle like a ghost
will wake inside the earth's still moving core
and shift the plates and cups I set today.
Or throw a body clear across the floor,
for wanting him like lava finds a way
to make an island tremor from the sea
and breach the quiet surface of my tea.

Distance

This is how I will enter you,
slip into you tonight,
thread my hands in yours,
wash your eyes with mine.

This is how I will take you
from inside—my legs, your legs
my mouth, your mouth
my heart, your heart.

This is how I will claim you
from that place we both know,
hold taut the thin line
from your distance to mine.

IV.

The River Blued

Where the pulse clinging to the rocks
Renews itself forever...
—O remember
In your narrowing dark hours
That more things move
Than blood in the heart.

—Louise Bogan

Twelve-Day Buddhist Silent Retreat

They fell in love while they were washing pots
and had no voices for twelve days—they had
watched each other through their meditations,
fallen deep into each other's fields.

On the twelfth day, they could speak with words again.

He was a boilermaker from Boston.
She, a Miami anthropologist.
He was married, with three children at home.
She had none, and was looking for someone.

He asked her then—What's anthropology?

She felt her voice in her throat like a live thing,
and she could only smile and laugh back
to the pots, huge and shiny in their hands,
reflecting their faces like children.

Event Horizons

Swallow

It may take one
tiny hollowed skeleton
on the stoop below—
for the eyes to rise and see
the swallows nesting
beneath the window.

Silences

In a small boat, the world
becomes big and wild again.
The weather is more than words,

but what you live your life by—
that loneliness you can touch
like a smooth tree you know,

but don't know the name of.

Thera

Why do we want to go
to the rim of that volcano
that spelled oblivion—
to lift her layered, dark hem
and touch the city lost again
beneath a wine-dark ocean?

Crossroads

My city drawn and quartered in this grid
of crossroad after crossroad, under bridges
stretched over parts of town that strobe the night—
a place to sell your soul at every stoplight.

Exposure

Ask any old poet—
you can die from it,
even after eating
your companions.

Legacies

If another poet has said it,
forget it—you can't. Even if the egret
was a twisted *S* the first time you saw it.
Even if you lived all those years with that taut
barbed wire catching—*Ich Ich*—in your throat.

Event Horizons

In the horizon surrounding a black hole,
the light trapped from the birth of the sun
circles the edge of its boundary cell—
history returning, ad infinitum.

After Basho

A rusted helmet—
beneath its dark mound, the night
song of a cricket.

History's *Stories*

For her song and flight, Echo is torn apart,   *art*
flung limb by singing limb. Each valley swallows,   *allows*
her voice. In another tale, a flame enchants   *chance*
encounters—Narcissus, who never returns,   *turns*—
her love to stone. Rocks, caves, dens, the hollow   *hollow*
of bones become her home—the old echoes,   *O's*
that round our inner lives like the concentric   *trick*
rings inside trees, reverberate for years,   *our ears*—
Our voices rise and leave, traveling,   *raveling, veiling*
currents across the sea, longing to reach   *each*
Atlantis, locate shapes that sounds recall—   *call*
back the world, as it was first encountered,   *heard*.

Catwalk

Come away, O human child!
To the waters and the wild
With a faery, hand in hand,
For the world's more full of weeping
than you can understand.
                    —W. B. Yeats

I leave the bed, as distant as the stars,
and reaching, find the doorway in the dark,
my bare legs long and cool like sudden roots.
A fan, forgotten, blowing up a storm,
and in the hallway I can almost hear
the murmuring of children in the room
beside ours. There are none, as yet, but that
is not the point. The full moon floods the night,
and quiet calls me out into the garden.
The wind against my skin the only thing
which can convince me he is gone. But no—
he's just inside, still sleeping like a child,

when all the spinning wheels begin to sing

and call my heart away—o human child,
o come away—the waters and the wild
are waiting for your heart to split in two,
are waiting, waiting for the rest of you
to recognize your spoken boundaries
mean nothing to the voices in these trees.
If you were still a child, you would ride
this flower like a bee—you'd climb inside.
But naked now, like this, you must admit,
your woman's body may no longer fit
the size and shape of this uncertain bloom
which only shows by night—a captive moon.

Circumstance

If she was recognized, she turned herself
into a tree, grew stories from her fingertips,
shook them off like bright, gold leaves in the wind.
Or she held them heavy, offered the fruit
for a new life—within inches, or miles,

if the right bird was there at the right time.

Her trees traveled in the bellies of birds,
flew great distances, allowed circumstance
of wind, of rain, of storm, of flight, or fire
to do the planting, place them in the ground,
in the dark soil of her ancestors.

Legacy

(for JFK Jr. 1960-1999)

Aegina—waking to the news on the radio
in Greek, so fast all I hear is your name
again and again—that terrible tone.
The long day's pause—awaiting confirmation.
How could we not collectively think
of a curse on your house? On Greek TV,
I see the photos of your childhood
framed by your father's desk and casket.
Across the ocean, Peruvians submerge
the pictures in the river to cleanse your name.
You seemed to be emerging from the hollows
of this century, somehow unscathed—Still,
you sought the skies' escape, like Icarus,
Phaethon, so many legendary children.
It was the legacy you couldn't trade
that brought you everything too early on—
a changeling sent at three into the sun.

Miami Beach

And all will be water again.
— (Cherokee)

My hometown was dredged from
the bottom of the ocean.

It is a skinny strip of land
the sea would have reclaimed,

but for the vigil of these walls
of barrier hotels.

Nights, if you sit along this shore,
your back to all the glamour,

you can see nothing but the way
we've come, and nothing but the way

to go.

Miami Circle

From the bay window of the room on the mezzanine,
we could see a circle appearing in the limestone.
We went below, where the archaeologists
were quietly sifting beneath the Tequesta statue,
thousands of people hurrying by for work,
hardly even aware they crossed a river.
The archaeologist said he used to live
in the building on this site, among the skyscrapers.
He never knew what lay beneath his room.

The Tequesta, or maybe the Mayans, left this circle
at the mouth of this river, the mouth of this continent.
He said the Tequesta believed we have three souls
residing in our eyes, reflections, shadows.
There were holes aligned to the two solstices
and the equinox. We entered the almanac,
the bones of a shark buried in its center,
the carved turtle, whale, the almond hole,
with a round rock like the iris of an eye.

Miami, my city hungry for history, for alignment—
Fitting this calendar should appear beneath our feet,
the charcoal dating at two thousand years.
(And they say down here that no one is from Miami.)
I was always running from home—to ruined Dresden,
to the high, quiet stones of Machu Picchu,
to the Island of the Moon in search of history.
We hardly know the things we might unearth
in our dismissed hometowns when we return,

the ghosts we might find at the mouths of our rivers.

Excavations

Only the slaves of Pompeii remain
preserved with the expressions held
when lava filled the town with force enough
to tear their limbs away. The library of skulls
contains the story—

But how will the historians explain
Hiroshima—for one—the black rain
that fused fingers to the bone,
the temporary survivors, terrified of their own
remaining limbs.

Geologic

A geologic second passed.
We waged a hundred thousand wars,
believing each to be the last—
our geologic second passed.

A new millennium—at last,
and deep within the planet's core,
another millisecond passed.
We wage a hundred thousand more.

The Harvest

The harvest happened here
say the fields of stumps, clear-
cut to the horizon.

Sawmills floated in.
Gridwork. Crossties. Engines. Rails.
Two men called a saw.

Thousand year olds dragged
over saplings, carved trenches
in the ghost forest.

Wheels grinding day and night.
The whistle shrilled—two long, one short
one long—Dead man call.

Isla de la Luna (Lago Titicaca, Bolivia)

Every year, on the twenty-first of June,
when the sun reached the top of Ilampu,
one woman knew she would be chosen—
her skin opened to the morning sun,
her blood caught and poured into the earth,
like the seeds of purple maize she had planted
every year, in rows, and grown for the *chicha*
the daughters she would never have would drink
with their granddaughters and theirs, years later—
at the slaughter of a bone-white llama,
the blood splashed at the dark entrances
of mines, to keep the holes from caving in.

Watermark

In every desert, travelers have dried up in the sun,
with shallow wells of water right below them.
Perhaps they left too soon, too young, too desperate to run
towards something or away from something else.

Perhaps they hadn't learned the way to read the tiny trails,
the watermarks remaining from a people who have gone,
whose hieroglyphs translate—in this direction is a spring
of sweet water. Look for it. Or is it, listen?

Poetry

I have to believe there is something
she is crying out for
when she cuts me like that.
I have to believe she needs
more than these walls.

I have to believe, one day, she will listen
for more than heels in the hall
or tongues around a corner,
and she will find out
what she has been so angry about

missing.

The River Blued

(after Mandelstam's 394)

Dragging one foot on a road she knows well,
setting the pace, she watches behind her,
her sister and that boy, one year older
or one year younger—it doesn't matter.

One part of her holds back, drives the other part on.
Revelation reminds her what she has lost,
but she is sure—that in between each breath,
there is somehow a resurrection.

There are women with rivers running through them.
They were born to ferry between
the living and the dead, to greet the resurrected.
They cannot be touched, and they cannot be left.

Angel, cocoon, metamorph—a white silhouette
on white. What grows out of this riverbank
is green, and we have someone's word
there is a waterwheel near here that turns.

Echolocations

The waters compassed me about, even to the soul:
the depth closed me round about,
the weeds were wrapped about my head.
                    —Jonah 2:5

In *Boca Vieja*, on the unsettled stretch of beach
which formed the border between two continents,
a coast where water flowed down from the forest—
I had come to find the furthest distance.
At the end of a labyrinth of fallen boulders,
I came upon the massive skeleton,
the whitened frame reflecting back the sun.
The ribcage formed a passage to the sea,
where thin rivers ran between the bones,
dividing further as they reached the ocean.
The skull, half-buried in the sand, resembled
a house from some forgotten fairy tale.
I climbed in through the porthole of an eye,
looked out the double circles filled with light.

I found my way down what was once her throat
and wandered through the gallery of bones.
Her ribcage framed the sea, the sky, the trees—
each canvas a vast range of blues and greens.
I reached the place that must have held her heart,
knowing, as a child, I could have fit inside
her vessels, even. I could have hidden there.
The tide was coming in, reclaiming things
clinging to the curved bones or roaming the shore—
the tiny hydroid forests with their medusae,
the limpets like small traveling volcanoes,
the scrolled whelks, drawing their maze of whorls,
only to be washed away. This was the end
of the whale's road. She passed her life to thousands.

I felt the sun-warm bone against my skin—
and a sudden heartbeat in the skeleton.
Her heart beat with a distant beckoning,
and in a moment I was with her, traveling
the *hwaelweg*, the road itself another kenning.
The ocean set the cadence, the swells singing
a line, receiving back another line—
in each reply, the slightest variation.
Our languages returning to the sounds
encoded in our strands, the spiral towers
of our helixes spinning round each other.
The calls reverberating through the waters
to navigate the depths, to guide us through
one ocean to another, the dark indigos,

the song returning from the deepest blues.

"Kinder- und Hausmärchen":
- original title of *Grimm's Fairy Tales*
- *Es war einmal im tiefen tiefen Wald*: Once upon a time in the deep deep wood

"Delineations":
- *Kind, du fragst mir Löcher im Bauch*: German idiom—Child, you ask me holes in my stomach.
- *Verfahr dich nicht*: Don't lose your way.

"Trümmerfrauen":
- rubble women

"Träume":
- dreams

"Crossing":
- *Da kommt man nimmer zum Grunde*: One would never reach the bottom. (In a letter to his son, Robinson Jeffers recalled, as a child crossing the Atlantic, hearing a German sailor speak these words.)

"Memento Mori in Middle School":
- *memento mori:* a reminder of mortality, or of humans' failures and mistakes
- *il miglior fabbro*: the better craftsman—Dante's term for Virgil

"Bedside Readers":
- *Terror Street and Agony Way, Love is a Dog from Hell:* books by Bukowski
- "This be the Verse" and "Talking in Bed": poems by Larkin

"Echolocations":
- *Boca Vieja*: (Old Mouth), Pacific Coast, Colombia
- *hwaelweg*: whale-road, Old English kenning

A Note About the Author

Diane Thiel's poetry appears in numerous journals and anthologies, including *Poetry*, *The Hudson Review*, *Best American Poetry 1999*, and *Beacon Best of 2000*. She has received several national poetry awards, such as the Robert Frost Award, the Robinson Jeffers Award, and the *New Millennium Writings* Award. She completed her B.A. and M.F.A. at Brown University in 1990. She is the author of two chapbooks from Aralia Press: *Cleft in the Wall* (1999) and a single-poem chapbook, *Echolocations* (2000). Her writing guide, *Writing Your Rhythm: Using Nature, Culture, Form and Myth*, is forthcoming from Story Line Press in 2001. She has taught at Brown University, Florida International University, and University of Miami—where she currently holds the Visiting Poet/ Assistant Professor position. She has traveled and lived in several countries in Europe and South America. She is fluent in Spanish, German, French, and speaks some Greek.

www.dianethiel.net

A Note About the Type

This book was set in Janson, a typeface long thought to have been made by the Dutchman Anton Janson, who was a practicing type founder in Leipzig during the years 1668–1687. However, it has been conclusively demonstrated that these types are actually the work of Nicholas Kis (1650–1702), a Hungarian, who most probably learned his trade from the master Dutch type founder Dirk Voskens. The type is an excellent example of the influential and sturdy Dutch types that prevailed in England up to the time William Caslon (1692–1766) developed his own incomparable designs from them.